The
TRIPLE CROWN
OF
Youth Baseball

Joey Anderson

TABLE OF CONTENTS

PREFACE

People ask me the same questions almost every season: What drives you to coach youth baseball year after year? Why do you volunteer your time to help others? How did you learn to do that? When are you going to write a book about your experiences to share with others? The answers are simple: (1) I love the game of baseball; (2) it's satisfying to see our youth show personal growth; (3) I learned through hard work, experience, and failures; and (4) your reading it right now!

As a young boy, baseball was an outlet for two hours that allowed me to escape everything else in my life that was circling around me like a shark. It enabled me to interact with my friends, stay out of trouble, and stay physically fit. It also allowed my personality to change from a shy, introverted kid in middle school who wouldn't interact with others, to the social, ambitious, energetic person I have become today.

I was inspired to write this book to help others avoid mistakes and improve their overall experiences. Through more than twenty-five years of playing, parenting, and coaching youth baseball, I have experienced a lot. With those experiences came joy, happiness, frustrations, heartache, and, best of all, memories. By sharing those experiences and the information I have obtained, I hope to help others create their own positive memories.

The Triple Crown is an award given to a Major League Baseball player who leads his respective league in the three main offensive categories: batting average, home runs, and runs batted in (RBIs). This award is prestigious because it has only been accomplished seventeen times in Major League history, most recently in 2012, by Miguel Cabrera of the Detroit Tigers. Cabrera was the first to win the Triple Crown since 1967, when Carl Yastrzemski accomplished the feat.

The reason I chose this title for my book was that, to me, the award and youth baseball are oddly similar. Like the Triple Crown award, I believe that there are three main components to youth baseball: players, parents, and coaches. When all three pieces come together and support one another you truly have something special. Almost every situation, player, parent, and coach is different, but the importance of the cohesiveness within the youth baseball's Triple Crown and its effect on athletic success is universal.

Triple Crown will take you back through some of my most memorable baseball experiences, both good and bad. It will give players of all ages measurable goals, and strategies for attaining them, to ensure they are maximizing their potential. It will also suggest specific ways to improve all aspects of their game.

Triple Crown is a guide to help parents navigate the journey and challenges their child may face as a player, from tee-ball to high school and beyond. I hope this book will give aspiring parents the tools to become a coach or an assistant at any level. It will also explain how to make baseball a rewarding and positive experience for your children even if you choose to be, as many of us are, their number-one fans.

Triple Crown is a user's guide for beginning, intermediate, and even "seasoned veteran" coaches. It provides insight into what I learned, how I failed, and my growth through the years with my two sons playing Little League, Babe Ruth baseball, travel ball, all-stars, and high school baseball.

During the journey of writing this book, I realized how important it is to give back instead of holding onto coaching secrets until the bitter end. Many of us live our lives never once stopping to think about how others have helped us or how we can give back. When we bid farewell to this world, our information and experiences will be wasted unless they have been shared.

I would like to thank the people instrumental to my writing this book. Foremost is my mom, Dawn. She is a woman who always pushes me to be the best I can be and loves her family unconditionally. She worked two, and sometimes three jobs to make sure we always had the things we needed and even things we didn't.

Next, I would like to thank my late grandmother, Sheryl "Mema" Hawk. As I was growing up, she was more than my grandmother; she was my second parent who made sure we ate our vegetables, did our homework, finished our paper route, and made it to every baseball practice and game on time. It was ironic that her last name was Hawk, because while my mom was working swing shift at the local hospital or headed to her second job, she really did watch over my sister, cousin, and I like a hawk.

Last but not least, I would like to thank my three kids, Kolby, Kordell, and Addison, who challenge me to be a better father each and every day. My beloved fiancée, Crystal, who has made me a better man since the day we met, and my sister, Amy, who has protected and counseled me as only a big sister can. Thank you all! Enjoy!

Service to others is the rent you pay for your room here on earth.

—Muhammad Ali

INTRODUCTION

As a player, have you struggled to improve from season to season or to become the best you can be? Do you lack the knowledge as a parent regarding the what, when, and how part of being a great baseball parent? Do you need help becoming more confident or lack the basic knowledge to become a coach in youth baseball? I offer this book with its suggestions to try to help with those issues and many, many more!

In this book, I will recommend ways to maximize your potential as a player by increasing your overall **M**ental Focus, **A**mbition, and **P**hysical Abilities (MAP) levels. You will also discover ways to increase your playing time at every level. Along the way, you will encounter this phrase "Triple Crown Tip." This phrase highlights helpful information that I have added for you, the reader. Keep an eye out for these tips! They will aid you during the reading of this book on how to become a more effective player, parent, and coach.

If you are seeking a "This is how I did it" memoir from a former Hall of Famer, Major League Baseball (MLB) player, or someone who battled his way through college and the minors to overcome insurmountable odds and achieve financial wealth, this book may not be for you. It contains real-life baseball stories from my experiences as a young boy, teenager, adult, player, parent, and coach.

Over the years, I have gone through it all—painful parent relationships, heartache, losses, mistakes, triumphant victories, successes, and failures. What I have found is that playing baseball, being a parent, and coaching youth baseball collectively comprise one of the most rewarding things I have ever done in my life.

Looking back, I absorbed some of the most valuable lessons of my life on the baseball field. I learned the importance of hard work and what it takes to be a competitor. I learned about failure, and how to respond with resilience, grit, and an attitude that fuels a determination to succeed. I experienced firsthand the principles of teamwork and the necessity of cohesion. I gained confidence in myself. And I also realized the critical importance of good leaders in life, both on and off the field. I was exposed to some great coaches, and some that were not so great. I spent countless hours with these men, and they had a tremendous amount of influence upon me during an impressionable phase of my youth. These experiences laid the foundations for the rest of my life, not only as an athlete, but also as a career professional, husband, and eventually a father.

The player, parent, and coaching facts, along with quotes, techniques, tips, tools, and stories you're about to read in the pages ahead may change the way you approach youth baseball. Each chapter provides new information that can help you prepare for just about every situation while gaining an advantage that others may not have. If you follow the advice I reveal in this book, it's possible you may enjoy your best seasons yet. What better time than *right now*? On to Chapter 1 ..

*If you have the opportunity in life to make things better,
and you don't, you're wasting your time on earth.*

—Roberto Clemente

CHAPTER 1: PLAYER

Creating Lasting Memories

It was the middle of August on a blistering ninety-degree summer day in 1989. We lived on a steep hill on the east side of Roseburg, a small but quiet town nestled along the I-5 corridor in Southern Oregon. My cousin, Chris, and I were told to go play outside for a while, as we had been doing most summer days. Keep in mind that during the '80s, playing outside was the norm, and so was drinking from a garden hose if you got too hot and thirsty.

One of our favorite areas to play was the driveway behind our house. We loved that area because, as I mentioned above, our house sat on a steep hill, and we had an even steeper driveway. This meant playing catch with a baseball in the front yard involved a risk. If one of us dropped the ball or missed it all together, it would go down the driveway. Then it would roll all the way to the street and another block or more before stopping.

It was an exhausting fifteen- to twenty-minute trip to retrieve the ball. In the summer, we used to say a baseball missed was donated to the neighborhood because nobody dared to chase after one in the heat of summer—much like the ball "Smalls" hit over the fence in the movie *The Sandlot*. The driveway that wrapped around the back of our house was graveled and narrow, front to back, but in our baseball-driven minds it was playable.

With the Little League baseball season in full swing, one of our favorite games to play was what we called "Strikeout." We would build a mound out of piled-up gravel and cut a home plate out of any thick corrugated cardboard, but sometimes all we could find was an old cereal box. Then, we took our positions, just like the positions we played in on our Little League team, I was the pitcher and my cousin was the catcher. The object of the game was for the pitcher to pitch the ball as if he were in a live game situation. If the pitcher threw three strikes, the batter was out. If he threw four balls and walked a batter, there was a ghost runner on first. This would continue until the pitcher struck out three batters. The catcher's job was to call the pitches as strikes or balls just as the umpire would normally do. If too many batters were walked, the other team would score runs, and we would lose the game. Sounds innocent enough, right? Well . . . not exactly.

On that summer day, my grandma, Mema, had parked the old Datsun right where we played Strikeout, so we had to move the mound and plate in front of our bedroom window. I started the game by throwing two hard fastballs on the inside corner. Each was bellowed out loudly by my cousin in his signature voice: "Steeerike!" As I started my windup for the third pitch, Chris explained to me that this batter was prone to chase the high fastballs and would be an easy out if I could place one upstairs a bit. As a kid in love with baseball and pitching, I followed my catcher's instructions. I started my windup with a high knee raise. As I reached back with my right arm, I thought, "If he wants the high heat, I will give it to him!" With a smooth follow-through, I released the ball, and as soon as it left my hand, a huge rush of adrenaline came over my body.

The ball sailed three feet over my cousin's head and crashed through our bedroom window, making a loud shattering noise, like a glass dropped on a hardwood floor. The next thing I remember was Mema yelling out the front door, "Joey Scott! Christopher! Get in here right now!" In case you're wondering, my middle name is Scott and my cousin's full name was Christopher. Like many parents tend to do, when my grandmother used those names instead of Joey or Chris, we were in serious trouble!

Before moving on to what happened next, I need to explain my Mema's role as the other parent in our upbringing. She had a heart of gold and would do anything to ensure our safety and happiness, but she was the enforcer at home while my mom was away. If she told us to do something, we did it, no questions asked. Back in the day, many enforcers had a yardstick or some type of paddle that hung on the wall. For Mema, when we saw her headed toward what we called the "Blue Flame," we knew what came next. This was an old, large, wooden pizza peel that my stepdad at the time had made for our kitchen. It was like the kind used in bakeries and pizza parlors to slide bread and pizzas into large-capacity ovens. It was painted light blue from end to end. We nicknamed it the Blue Flame because when my grandmother gave us the spankings we so deserved, it felt like our backsides were literally on fire.

As my cousin and I strolled toward the front door, we knew what lay ahead for both of us. Before Mema said anything, I quickly took the blame, as I was the one to throw the baseball through the window. She wasn't buying it one bit. "You both played catch with a hard ball in the backyard in front of the window, so you will both be punished," she said.

We nodded our heads in agreement because she had already told us several times not to play catch behind the house.

That night we lay in our beds awake, staring at the ceiling, both of us waiting for the other to speak first. I finally whispered over to my cousin, "If you would have caught the ball, dummy, we wouldn't have gotten in trouble."

He whispered back, "Yes, and if you would have thrown the pitch where I told you to, Nolan Ryan, it wouldn't hurt to sit on our backsides for the next couple of days!" After that, we both remained silent until we fell asleep. There was nothing else to say because we both knew that given the opportunity, we would be right back out there playing catch the next day, even in the same spot, if necessary.

This is just one of my many memories of playing baseball as a kid. It wasn't always the practices, games, or tournaments that created lasting memories; it was the pure fun of the game. It didn't matter to us that we were spanked for breaking the window. Sure we felt bad, but the joy of the game was worth it to us.

What more could a kid ask for than to grab a small leather ball with stitching and go play catch with a glove? Even now, I love baseball because it allows me to forget about the mundane concerns of everyday life. It also lets me spend time with youth players as a coach, and parents who take pleasure in enjoying a similar pastime. After all, as Yogi Berra said, "Love is the most important thing in the world, but baseball is pretty good too."

What made me fall in love with baseball—second to the fun involved—was the competitive nature of the game. By *competitive*, I mean the fight for playing time among teammates. Let's be honest; nobody ever says, "Let's go sit on the bench." No, they say, "Let's go play baseball."

Most beginning programs like tee-ball, Little League, Babe Ruth baseball, and Pony League require coaches to give equal playing time. By the time they reach middle school age, however, the equal-playing-time rule normally ends. Some players have more natural ability, and some practice more intensely to develop physical abilities. Players who have developed strong skills are rewarded with more playing time. If we didn't keep score, even at the lowest level (tee-ball) of recording outs, or the highest level of runs being scored (high school), what would drive players to work hard and improve? There is a reason we keep score: to drive teams to be competitive. It doesn't always mean we have to win or that the only reason we keep score is to be the best every time. It is part of the process of assessing capabilities, just like in school—not all students receive the same academic grades or the same amount of stage time in a play, or get to sit in the first seat of the brass or woodwinds section in band. Normally in all of these situations, the child who excels, practices hard, and listens to their teacher receives some type of reward. Just as in baseball, the player who works hard, listens to his coach, and practices hard normally receives more playing time.

There's no single logical explanation for how coaches hand out playing time, is there? In the best of all worlds, the coach is fair, and playing time is a reward for having a good attitude, displaying a winning effort, being a team player, making improvements, and displaying skill. Unfortunately, in middle and high school sports, you will rarely find the best of all worlds! If you're looking for an additional edge as a player, I recommend reading my Top 10 list below on how to increase your playing time at any level of youth baseball.

My Top 10 List—How to Increase Your Playing Time

1. **Appearance**: Dress for success. Each year before our first practices, I discuss the dress code for all players at our parent/team meeting. I require players to wear baseball hats, baseball-style shirts, pants, cleats, and a protective cup to all practices. Many have questioned this requirement, but the answer is always the same: all players are required to wear the proper clothing and equipment. A coach should push this at all levels. When a parent or player questions any of these items, I would suggest you use the following responses:

   - **Baseball hats**: These are always worn during a regular game, so why would you not wear a hat during practice?

Hats also help shade your line of vision to the baseball while trying to catch it (i.e., a fly ball, line drive, etc.).

- **Baseball-style shirts and pants**: These are always worn during a regular game as well. When you practice in a baseball-style shirt, you get a really good sense of what it will feel like during the game if you already wear it consistently at every practice. Conversely, if a pitcher practices throwing a bullpen session of fifty pitches in a tank top and shorts and then throws fifty pitches wearing his or her uniform in a live game the next day, the difference is night and day. The restrictive nature of the clothing is hard to emulate unless you are actually wearing it.

- **Cleats**: The proper shoes are a must. Have you ever tried to run a marathon in high heels? No! (If you answered yes, please send me the video. I would love to see that!) Then why would a player try to run a full sprint without wearing plastic or metal cleats that provide traction in the dirt or grass? When grass or dirt becomes wet, it is very dangerous for players to be wearing tennis shoes. I made this a mandatory item after a player at practice slipped rounding a base while wearing tennis shoes and broke his forearm in three places. Trust me, the conversation with a parent after a player is seriously injured is not something you want to have. That is especially the case if the injury could have been prevented, and you, as the coach, were ultimately responsible for their well-being.

- **Protective cup**: You would think this one is self-explanatory, but kids and parents shy away from it because players say it's uncomfortable. I have witnessed some ugly plays when it comes to a hard ball hitting a player in the groin. It's a situation that every coach needs to try to avoid. If you're going to coach youth baseball, the number-one priority as a coach is and always will be *safety*! By teaching your players why it's important to wear all of their protective equipment, you are helping them. As a player, wearing all of these items shows your coach that you respect his or her rules, are ready to play, and you're not going to waste their time or the team's.

Triple Crown Tip: As a parent, making sure they get to practice on time with all of these tools, including their glove, bat, batting gloves, helmet, and other important equipment, can only support your child's efforts.

2. **Put out maximum effort**: Show maximum effort in everything you do. Never take a play off, even if you know nobody is watching. A few examples are running out a routine ground ball or completing warm-up throws while the coach is meeting with an assistant. As a coach, when I see a player putting out maximum effort it tells me they care and want the opportunity to play. You may not be the most gifted athlete in the world, but if you give me more than the other guy does, I will notice it and reward those efforts.

3. **Have a positive attitude**: Baseball can discourage even the strongest of minds. I look for players who can handle the stress of small tasks and still maintain a good attitude

8

regardless of whether they fail or succeed. As the late, great Yogi Berra once said, "Baseball is 90 percent mental, and the other half is physical." I could not agree with him more. Yes, this is not a typo. His point was not to defy the basic concepts of mathematics, but to emphasize how success in baseball requires tremendous mental stamina. The great players are those who are able to handle failure and press on. Without a positive attitude, you will struggle with the mental part of anything. In baseball, a negative attitude can impact your performance and even your teammates.

4. **Be a supportive teammate**: I'm always looking for players who are great teammates. To be a great teammate, you have to care about the other players on your team and their success. This isn't a player who pats somebody on the back after he does one thing right or cheers a teammate on in the last inning because the team needs a hit to win the game. No, this is a player who may have more talent than the next guy but makes an effort every time to help others improve. It's also a player who stands up for others when doing so isn't popular among peers. The old motto "We win as a team, and we lose as a team" is exactly right. A great teammate encourages others when they succeed and picks them up when they fall. These are the types of qualities that help players become more valuable to the team.

5. **Be an effective communicator**: Communication is the real sign of leadership; I truly believe you simply can't become a great leader until you are a great communicator. Great communicators inspire others to perform better. They create

a connection that is real, emotional, and personal. Great communicators forge this connection through an understanding of people and an ability to speak directly to their needs in a manner that they are ready to hear. Active listening is a simple technique that ensures people feel heard, an essential component of good communication. To practice active listening, a youth player should spend more time listening than talking.

6. **Be prepared to learn something new**: Come to every practice hungry to learn more about baseball. Show the desire to absorb as much as you can each day. When I see players who only seem to care about the positions on the field where they think they should play, I try to change that mindset immediately. I like to teach all players that being prepared for game situations means knowing not only your position, but also everybody else's position on the field. For example, if you are a second baseman, then it is crucial to learn the responsibilities of the shortstop so you know where your teammate will be on any given play. As an infielder, even knowing the responsibilities of the coinciding outfield positions can be extremely valuable. With that information, you can be in the right location for cutoff throws, communication about fly balls, and so on.

7. **Maintain focus at all times**: Many baseball practices are dedicated to physical training or position-specific skills. The ability to focus, relax, and perform at the highest level is directly related to an athlete's mental approach. So how can baseball players establish and maintain mental focus? In

baseball, mental focus is the key to success at all levels. The team that has the better focus and mental approach usually wins in the end. For example, coaches must be able to teach players what should happen during each pitch or game situation. Players must know their specific role on every pitch in every situation. If you don't know your responsibilities when the game is in motion, then ask your coach to explain it when it's not. The ability to focus on each pitch comes from years of practice and learning.

Triple Crown Tip: The best professional players in the world are able to proactively visualize the next play on the field. Others just react when it happens. What type of player are you?

8. **Listen and ask relevant/productive questions**: I always tell my players that being a great listener is essential for learning. To learn, you have to listen. To grow, you have to listen, and when you grow, you become a better player and person.

   In addition to listening well, I feel it's important to ask productive questions. If a player were to be silent at every practice, I would instantly be worried. Always ask your coach if you don't understand what he or she is trying to explain, even if it means asking before or after practice. The timing of a question is key. Asking your coach if you can pitch at practice in the middle of a team drill is not a productive question and will likely deter your coach from ever allowing you to pitch. A productive question would be, "Hey, Coach, can you please explain the shortstop's responsibilities on a line drive to centerfield with a runner on second and only one out in an inning?"

9. **Follow instructions, and apply what you learn**—one of the best feelings as a coach is seeing players apply what they have learned. That is the proverbial "aha" lightbulb moment. To achieve this, a player should follow instructions during practice, learn from his or her mistakes, and apply what they learned. As the coach, you can usually tell who is listening and following instructions during practice or conditioning. As a player, a good way to make sure you are absorbing and retaining information is to maintain eye contact and stay close enough to your coach or instructor to hear every word they are saying. Even if you think the information they are covering is a review for your skill level, pay attention. You will likely be able to apply what you hear, making it valuable at some point.

Triple Crown Tip: I often ask questions at the end of practices to test my players on what they learned that day. The ones who know the correct answers are the ones who paid attention. If any player struggles with the answers to a question, we openly discuss it so that everyone leaves practice with a clear understanding of what we just covered. I use this time to evaluate myself as well. If a player doesn't learn something at the speed of others or I don't get my point across, then I need to make an adjustment during my next delivery of the information. This helps me as a coach to learn as the players are learning. It's a win-win.

10.   **Show respect for the game**: If you want to be a clown, go join the circus! During a recent local recreational league game, I witnessed a player personify lack of respect for the game to a T. The player was up to bat. He never really got set in his batting stance, and when he finally did, he made a total spectacle of himself. When this player got on base, he was thrown out on a force play at second base to end the inning because he did not push himself to hustle and was unwilling to slide. On the way back to the dugout, he argued with the field umpire excessively. After that half inning was finally over and the teams flipped sides, I spotted the same player at shortstop. While warm-up grounders were being thrown to each infield position, he was joking around by throwing the ball back to first base in an almost completely underhand motion.

The inning started with the other team's leadoff man hitting a screaming double to the left centerfield wall. During the play, the shortstop wasn't in the correct position to receive the cutoff throw. As the pitcher was getting ready to throw the next pitch, the runner on second took a standard lead. As the runner focused on the pitcher's motion, the shortstop came up right behind him on his left hip and proceeded to slap the glove right in his ear hole.

I realize many coaches teach the glove slap to distract the runner, but this was not one of those tactics. The kid was putting his glove right up to the opponent's ear hole in his helmet and slapping it repeatedly—to the extent that the umpire gave him a warning. This is a perfect example of poor sportsmanship; he is someone who has a win-at-all-cost attitude, only hustles when he feels like it, and puts himself before his team. I would encourage all players reading this book to never be that guy, or clown, on the field. By *clown*, I mean the person who wants everybody's attention and will create unnecessary distractions that ultimately hurt their team during games.

Not only did the situation reflect badly on the player, but it also reflected badly on the coach for allowing that type of behavior, and the parent for not instilling the importance of hard work ethic, being a good sport, and being respectful to officials.

I recommend coaches require the following of their players to teach them to show proper respect toward an opponent and themselves:

- Showing respect to the umpires and other team when entering the batter's box (i.e., tipping their cap to the catcher/umpire and minimizing movement while in the batting stance).

- Showing hustle between the foul lines — players should run out everything when the baseball is in play (i.e., ground balls and fly balls while on offense or being in the right position to receive a teammate's cutoff throw).

- Sliding whenever it's a close play. This is not only a great way to increase the chance of being safe at a base, but it can also prevent players from getting injured. In some leagues it is a requirement to slide, and the runner will be called out if they do not slide, especially at home plate.

- Showing respect to opponents. Slapping a glove directly in the ear hole of another player won't gain you any respect. As an infielder, hustling behind a base runner every time they take a lead so they can't steal, will keep the runner close.

Respect for the game in youth baseball, to me, means that everyone involved, from players to coaches, parents, fans, and officials, should conduct themselves according to the etiquette (sportsmanship) of the game. Keeping that in mind, everyone should be treating others with respect by never making the situation about oneself instead of about the game. Coaches have the responsibility to act with respect, teach players what respect means, and talk to the parents when that respect has been violated.

When do you know that respect for the game has been compromised? I think the answer is this: when people leave the field talking about incidents that are unrelated to the baseball playing itself, there is a problem.

Baseball is about talent, hard work, and strategy. But at the deepest level, it's about love, integrity, and respect.

—Pat Gillick

Another way I suggest to increase your overall playing time is to improve what I like to call the players' MAP: **M**ental focus > **A**mbition > **P**hysical abilities

Mental Focus

When I talk about mental focus in baseball, to me it's a little different than in other youth sports. My idea of a mentally focused baseball player is one who is calm and has a focused sense of self-worth and belief. As a hitter, you go up to the plate knowing you are going to make solid contact, not hoping to. As a fielder, you see yourself make a clean play, instead of standing back waiting for the ball to come to you and hoping you don't miss it. Pitchers with mental focus believe in every pitch they throw. They throw a 3-2 curveball or slider with the game on the line, and everyone, including the hitter, is expecting the fastball.

Players that lack self-confidence and mental focus can be exposed rather quickly. Just as players who truly believe in themselves and know, not hope, that they will get the job done tend to succeed at a much greater rate than those who don't.

A player should stay focused on the process (write down their goals and how they can work toward accomplishing them—nothing is a goal until you write it down). Goals are what hold them accountable. They should ask themselves, did I accomplish what I wrote down? If not, why didn't I achieve the goal? Did I put out max effort? If they didn't, change something, learn from it, and attack it again!

I suggest players set daily goals that help them refocus each day. Some of these goals could include: work on hitting off-speed pitches, when to take a pitch and when to be aggressive at the plate, practice dirt-ball reads to improve base running, studying your defensive position and how to react in every scenario. This can help them focus on what they need to improve on from the mental side of the game.

Here is an example of a plan I used last season with one of my players regarding hitting and increasing mental focus:

1. Establish a pre-game routine that allows you to be mentally prepared. While in the dugout, look through the hole in the top of your batting helmet and focus on the opposing pitcher to pick up his or her release point, determine if he or she is giving away clues as to what pitch is going to be thrown next, and gain all the information you can.

2. Establish a routine before each time up to bat that allows you to focus (e.g., breathing, focusing on where you want to hit the ball, what will you do if the ball comes in tight on you).

3. Have a plan at the plate based on the score, number of outs, inning, and any specific situation (e.g., being aggressive on a two ball and one strike count or taking a pitch on a three ball and no strike count). Always stay in the game mentally.

4. "Hammerin'" Hank Aaron said he could consistently hit the baseball because of his visualization and focus. Aaron is a great example of how mental preparation and visualization can yield powerful results. His mental focus took him to the baseball hall of fame.

5. Experience through practice and competition leads to knowledge, which gives you the confidence and power to be mentally ready for any situation. Repeat the same process at practice. *Do not* wait until game day! I like to tell my players at the beginning and end of every practice, "Practice how you want to play!"

6. Practice how you want to play. Treat every at bat during batting practices as if you are in a live game situation. If you're not concentrating enough in practice to hit a line-drive base hit, then it's likely you won't be mentally ready to during the game.

Triple Crown Tip: Try using visualization techniques before, during, and after games and practices. When you do something good, such as making solid contact and feeling good after an at bat, you must capture that feeling like you took a mental picture. Keep as much detail as possible stored in your mind. After the game or practice is over relive that moment in the car ride home. This will force your body to reproduce great performances because it will be programmed to do so.

Ambition

The true definition of ambition is to have a strong desire to do or to achieve something, typically requiring determination and hard work. I believe this is one of the most important characteristic traits in youth baseball players. Here are a few items I encourage players to think about:

- Set high expectations for yourself. I've seen players who perform above their school grade level. I've seen players who can do things adults deem impossible. All of this happens merely because the player believes he or she can. Set the bar high and always work hard to try to reach it. Once you reach it, set it higher. It is important not to become complacent in your abilities.

- Maintain high expectations for yourself, and even if you miss, you can end up at a higher level than if you kept your expectations low. This mind-set will breed ambition. Starting with low expectations of yourself and then trying to turn it on like a light switch can be a hard thing to do. Again, it takes a lot of hard work to stay on top and maintain something good. Be ready to keep pushing yourself!

- Don't be afraid to fail sometimes. Losing stinks, as every adult knows. Because of that, certain groups advocate encouraging self-esteem to the extent that the concept of "losing" is removed from the player's mind. Some baseball games no longer keep score. The challenges of little consequence are removed, all in the name of promoting players' self-worth. The result of this is that when life does deliver challenges that have consequences, the players' mental muscles aren't ready for the strain. Prepare yourself to become familiar with the strain needed for true success, and if you fail sometimes, so be it. Learn from loss and develop the skill set that comes with critical evaluation of performance. In doing so, you will learn how to bounce back from a loss and to know the self-esteem that comes from true achievement, not false accomplishment. Going through the growth process can change you as a player. If handled correctly, it can be the fuel that keeps the ambitious fire lit.

- Follow your dream. My youngest son wants to be a professional fishing guide, social entrepreneur, and adventurer. The adult in me wants to say his dream is not realistic. But I do realize this sort of dreaming represents him setting a high goal for himself. Sure, the odds of him becoming the next pro angler or Mark Zuckerberg in the world are roughly one in seven billion. Don't worry about counting the cost now. There will be time enough for that later. For now, I encourage you all to pursue those dreams with all your heart. As a player, believe in your dreams. Whether in baseball or in life, you must be ambitious to accomplish something great. We live in a fast-paced life where the successful people live in the left lane. Put your blinker on, change lanes, and get out there! (Please wait until you have a driver's license.)

- Have a +1 mentality. While my son may dream of being the best fishing guide ever, and I expect big things of him, I also know that buying him a boat right now to go out and start fishing would be useless. On the other hand, I do encourage him to get out on the water with an experienced guide and learn the tricks of the trade. This lets him feel the challenge is within reach. In whatever it is for your child, encourage them to be a tiny bit better than they were before. The accumulation of these constant small increases, regardless of the area of study, will lead to steady growth and increased ambition.

- Concentrate on effort, not results. Gains are accomplished through effort—really hard effort. You can't always win, but we can give our best effort. This is true whether in the deadlift squat, algebra, or how to cook a perfect steak. If you're a player who tries with all they have, regardless of the outcome, give yourself a high five. At the same time, if you're a player who doesn't try, then believe me, as a coach, we can pick up on it really fast. As a coach, I don't like to put players down, but I do like to encourage them to try harder next time, and I let them know I support them. I encourage players to analyze what went wrong and consider how they can prevent it from happening again.

Starting your kid down the path of believing they can accomplish anything if they work hard enough will do far more for their baseball experience than instilling a belief that they just have talent. The belief in one's ability to accomplish anything through hard work will carry over into many other parts of life. Praise effort first. You'll notice I will mention this several times over the next chapter, only because I believe it's very important.

Physical Abilities

So we have talked about the mental focus part and having the ambition to accomplish something great. You may be asking yourself, "Isn't that enough?" No, I believe it's not. If you have mental focus and ambition but lack the physical abilities that others have, then you may be fighting an uphill battle.

I feel that if any of these three components are missing you can be out of balance and the results won't be at the level you're trying to achieve. Think about it this way. Does a player that has all of the physical skills in the world succeed when they lack mental focus or the ambition to get better through hard work? Does a player that pays attention all the time and has a positive attitude succeed at the physical parts of baseball? Hopefully you answered no to both of those questions. The reason I say that is because without all of those things it's very hard to maximize your potential as a player. I do think you can use one or two of the components to help you increase the others.

I believe a player's physical abilities aren't just something they are born with. I think they're something that can be changed. If you put in the time and effort your fundamental skills and physical abilities should increase.

With that being said, if you would like to move from being an average youth baseball player to becoming a great player, you must put the time in through training your body to perform better. I'm not saying that to play youth baseball you have to go work out like a professional athlete does, but if your goal is to actually improve, you have to condition your body. In order to obtain some type of physical gain, you must sweat!

Do you work on throwing in the off-season? Do you jog or run several miles three to four times per week? How many ground balls or fly balls do you catch before or after the season? If the answers to those questions are all no/none, then you may be lying to yourself and aren't fully invested in improving. The majority of players I see who go on to play high school baseball and beyond are working out in the off-season, going to training camps, and so on.

One of the best ways to improve your physical abilities is one that most people don't think of first. Actually, when talking to the parents of youth players it's generally not even second or third behind practicing with their team or getting private lessons. Although those things can be important, I feel that practicing at home is even more important. It can be with Mom, Dad, or even an older sibling.

Nothing gets me more excited than for a player to come to a practice and say they threw over the weekend with a friend or family member. In fact, over the years I have seen players who have an older sibling involved in baseball or a supportive parent, and they are the ones whose physical abilities usually improved the most.

Players, grab your glove or mitt, and go play catch!

> *There are three types of baseball players: those who make it happen, those who watch it happen, and those who wonder what happened.*
>
> —Tommy Lasorda

CHAPTER 2: PARENT

As a parent, you may face many challenges during youth baseball in terms of which path to take. Do I start my son in the local recreational league? Should I have him play on a travel or club team? What are the pros and cons of paying for private lessons? These are just a few of the questions parents ask me every year.

In my opinion, there is no wrong answer to those questions. I believe as long as your youth baseball player is creating lasting memories while having fun, learning the fundamentals while learning the game, and growing to reach his or her maximum potential, you can choose one of many paths. In other words, playing in a recreational league at a young age and later deciding to join a travel team is not a bad decision. Neither is keeping your kid in a local baseball club or playing in a summer league and exploring other avenues when you feel the time is right. Most importantly, choose the path that will give your player the best possible baseball experience.

Children play sports because they enjoy the experience. Adults play the same game because they enjoy it. Professional athletes play the sport they chose because they love to play, and when it stops being enjoyable they usually retire. For me the same is true, but there was one moment in time that sticks out: a moment when I fell in love with the game of baseball.

As a youngster, my most memorable experience watching baseball was on a summer trip with my mom to Seattle. She bought us tickets to a Seattle Mariners MLB game at the Kingdome. It was my first time attending a professional baseball game. When she initially told me we were going to the game, I nearly fainted from the shock and excitement. After a six-hour drive up I-5 from Roseburg, we finally climbed over the final hill past Tacoma, Washington, and there it was. I saw not only the Kingdome but also several really tall skyscrapers and the Puget Sound streaming along the background. It was a magnificent sight. Keep in mind this was my first exposure to any type of big city. I was born in the small town of Galesburg, Illinois, and grew up in Roseburg, Oregon, so the two cities combined weren't over fifty thousand people total. The greatest part about this section was that traffic was heavy, forcing my mom to drive very slow. With my face glued firmly to the window, I got to take in all of the scenery.

After passing through the enormous gates at the entrance to the Kingdome, we proceeded to the main walkway and the stadium seating. As we headed toward the seating entrance, the sights and smells were overwhelming: the distinct aroma of roasted peanuts passing by on a tray carried by vendors filled the air, plump hot dogs turning on old-style dog broilers, and fresh popcorn popping loudly in a hot oil popper easily distracted my senses. We stopped and grabbed one of each and the largest fountain sodas we could carry. With our drinks and delicious concession food, we walked through the numbered gate and proceeded to find our seats.

After sitting down in my seat, I looked up and was at a loss for words. What I saw that day was truly breathtaking. The Mariners' team colors of navy blue, metallic silver, northwest green, and white blanketed everything from the stadium seats to the outfield padding. As the Mariners took the field, I was completely starstruck. Dave Valle settled in behind home plate to receive the warm-up pitches from none other than the Mariners' ace in 1992, "the Big Unit," Randy Johnson. My mom described him as a very tall, skinny, stringy-haired man. To this day, her description of the now hall of famer still makes me laugh inside.

The next two players I noticed were Edgar Martinez and "the Kid," Ken Griffey. From the first time I laid eyes on those two players, I knew they were something very special. I would spend most of my childhood and teenage years pretending to be them while playing Wiffle ball at home or home-run derby at Gaddis Park, our local Little League fields.

With a great pitching performance from Randy Johnson, the Mariners went on to beat the Minnesota twins that day. I learned so much about baseball by watching the game that day and had the time of my life in the process. Looking back, this is, without a shadow of doubt, the day I fell in love with the game of baseball.

My mom, she wasn't like a baseball mother who knew everything about the game. She just wanted me to be happy with what I was doing.

—David Ortiz

PARENT AND PLAYER RELATIONSHIP

As it relates to youth baseball, I have noticed some trends that concern me among parents and their relationships with their children.

1. Some parents aren't realistic about their child's talent.

2. A few struggle to separate the emotions they feel during the game from those of their child.

3. A small portion find it necessary to inject their opinions and/or suggestions for the team because they pay money to be part of the organization.

4. Occasionally parents severely hinder their child's progress and passion for the sport they play. Some of these excuses include but are not limited to the following: the child has been sick, he or she didn't get enough sleep, they forgot their contact lenses, their new cleats don't fit right, the new glove they bought isn't broken in yet.

Here are some suggestions and proposed solutions to what I've described above. I will explain why these may be necessary for your player to enjoy the game of baseball and hopefully not hate you by the time they are eighteen years of age.

1. Your child will only go as far as the love they have for what they do. This applies not only to baseball, but also to life in general. Support what they love and are interested in, not what you think they should be involved in. You had a childhood; now please let your child have theirs.

2. You may not have been that good (i.e., in high school sports). Most parents have a fixed mindset that they excelled in the sport they competed in during high school. However, hindsight is 20/20. In the grand scheme of things, were you really that good?

3. Leave your child alone during competition. Your child is out on the field competing and does not need any added pressure from you telling them what they should or should not do. Try saving it for the car ride home, and if it is not constructive, keep it to yourself. Your insights on their performance are usually driven by emotion and passion and typically come off as confrontational. This is an excellent way to kill the joy and desire to keep playing.

4. Please let the coaches do the coaching. Did you sign up to coach this year? Did you volunteer your time away from your family to help others? Yes, you may have coached in a recreational league or travel club in the past, but that in no way allows you the right to give the coach suggestions regarding lineup, playing time, and direction for the team. As a parent your opinion is valued, but it is the coach's decisions that will ultimately affect your player's overall experience. Setting up a time before or after practice and games is usually the best time to ask questions or voice any concerns you may have. Again, these should be realistic concerns or questions. Like, what could I do to help my player improve their overall batting, or what should I do to help them catch fly balls, or what do you suggest I do to improve their

pitching capabilities. If your player is not getting the playing time you think they deserve, the question should be, "What can I do to help increase my player's time on the field?"

5. Let your child enjoy the process. Sports are a never-ending process of learning, both social and fundamentally. There's an inherent value to the social and fundamental aspects of sports, and the early years of athletics can be unbelievably valuable for your child's social skills in the future.

People often ask what my parents' role was when I played youth baseball. I tell those people that my mom and grandma were supportive of my love of baseball and gave me every opportunity to succeed. Whether I played a great game or a terrible game, my mom and Mema always treated me with the same support and love. They never pushed me in any way, and anything that I accomplished was because of my own ambition and their support. They had complete trust in my coaches, and I was very lucky to have some good ones along the way. So when you look at your child and you see an MLB player, understand that they may view themselves differently. Parents: please don't be the reason for your child's failures; again, they're under enough pressure already.

My mother and grandma's role was getting me to practice and games on time or even a few minutes early, making sure I had everything I needed to be successful at practice, not making excuses to my coach about my poor performance in a game or practice, and listening when I had something bothering me.

Below are the ten types of parents I usually experience each year. This section of the book may shock you, make you laugh, or even surprise you, but I challenge you to read each of them with an open mind. Then ask yourself which parent you are.

My "10 Types of Parents" List

1. The Pro Parent: This type of parent usually thinks that because they played high school baseball back when corn lined the outfield, they know everything there is to know about the game and how to coach their player today. They also constantly interject before, during, and after all practices and games. I have seen parents who once reached the MLB level yet are out of their element at a practice trying to coach a youth baseball team. Being a former big-league player does not always guarantee you will be a good coach. Why? If you are lucky to make it to the professional level (roughly 1 percent chance), you will be interacting with people that are between the ages of twenty years old and forty years old (adults). Those people are then working and being paid to play the game of baseball. Now think about how that relates to youth baseball. It doesn't; they are polar opposites, which makes it hard to relate to or even coach youth players.

2. The Emotional Parent: This parent wants to make sure he or she tells you all about their child's skills and accomplishments before you even get on the practice field. They offer to do anything they can to help the team if it means that preferential treatment is given to them

and their child (i.e., a chance to pitch, bat first in the lineup, play every inning of all the games, etc.). Last but certainly not least, this parent typically criticizes other players to make their own child look better.

3. The Competitive Parent: This parent is most concerned with winning, and sometimes even that's not good enough. They will support scoring extra runs when a team has the game in hand. For instance, this parent would encourage an extra inning be played even if the ten-run mercy rule was in effect just so their child could score one more run, get one more hit, or strike out one more batter. The competitive parent may talk to the coach about things he or she thinks should be done so the team can win. They want to see the team win, and they would like to offer their coaching "expertise" to help them out. Do you see the pattern developing here? Everything is centered around the word *WIN*.

4. The Living-Through-Your-Kids Parent: This parent sometimes forces their child into playing the sport they played and loved without even asking whether the child shares the same feelings about baseball. All while trying to relive their childhood and the glory days of youth sports. Each time his or her kid steps into the batter's box it is a life or death moment. The parent gets so fired up, pacing back and forth and barking instructions at their child, that other parents have contemplated bringing a tranquilizer gun to the game, "just in case." When their child plays outfield, you'll see them loitering along the

fence behind center field. And if their player doesn't get as much playing time as another kid, the coach is going to get an ear full.

5. The "Blame Game" Parent: This is a parent who tends to blame others and points the finger at someone else for why their child didn't play well or misbehaved. They typically will not look at a situation and take responsibility for themselves. Even under the most obvious circumstances this parent will defend their stance till the bitter end. For example, this parent blames the team for not scoring enough runs in a game that their son or daughter pitched in as the reason for the team losing. Overlooking the fact that the team played really well overall and lost the game 4-3 in extra innings.

6. The Superstar Kid Parent: This parent believes their child has superior talent compared to other players on the team, and is looking for special treatment from coaches. They also feel that their child should play every inning, only pitch or play shortstop (the child's favorite positions), and bat at the top of the order. This could be the parent who starts a travel ball team so they can be in control of their child's playing time (a.k.a. Daddy Ball). I believe you're not doing him or her any good. Competition usually promotes growth. If they are not competing in traditional team dynamics, they're going to find out the hard way when they get to the level where Daddy and Mommy aren't allowed around anymore.

7. The Blasé Parent: This parent leans toward agreeing with everything you say. They usually don't ask questions and only want their kids to have fun—there is not one competitive bone in their body. The words, "That's fine with me," or "Sure, no problem" is often spoken by this parent. This parent tends to drop their player off, leaves, and then sits in the car when they come to pick them up. The blasé parent can be frustrating to work with as a coach, because they show no interest, are sometimes unreliable, and don't make baseball a priority. If it doesn't fit in their schedule, they sometimes don't see that it is a big deal that their player will have to miss practice.

8. The Outspoken Parent: The outspoken parent typically responds to every text message, email, or post that you send out to the team/parents. They will not hesitate to make a scene at a practice or game until they get your attention or an answer. They tend to find it necessary to challenge everything to feel involved. The outspoken parent is a wildcard. This parent can be both good and bad. If dealt with effectively, they can be a valuable parent to have on your team.

9. The Critical Parent: This parent is the one who yells at their child if they do one thing wrong on the baseball diamond or at the umpire over one call. The parent usually demands more: "Why aren't you running fast enough to the base?" "Why didn't you catch that fly ball?" "If you don't try harder next time, I'm going to

have your coach put you on the bench!" This parent can kill the fun of the game for any child. Baseball is a game of failure, and we need to teach these young players how to bounce back from a bad day at the park and building confidence is the best way to do that. Life has a lot of bad days sometimes too. Wouldn't you love for your kid to come out of a bad day with a good attitude that tomorrow will be better?

10. The Model Parent: Most of the time this parent gets their player to practice at or before the exact time of practice and games. This parent's player is normally respectful to the coaches, other players, and umpires without you needing to say anything. He or she offers to help with practice but isn't pushy at any point. This parent thanks you for volunteering your time and efforts in coaching all the players. They also help others to support the team's overall goals. The model parent is a dream. They make your job as a coach so much easier. Their kids are generally the easiest to coach, they support the team's goals, and they have a genuine interest in seeing everyone on the team succeed. This tends to be my favorite parent, for obvious reasons.

Now that you have read them all, which parent are you? Seeing this from a coach's perspective, does this change your outlook at all?

I know while writing this section it opened my eyes. As a parent and spectator of my oldest son playing high school baseball, I have been ALL of these parents at one point or another. It took some learning along the way to make the necessary changes, but I did it to insure I wouldn't follow the same path while coaching my youngest son.

As a parent of a young baseball player, it's easy to let the crazy nature of a season get in the way of the big picture. Below are my top 10 suggested tips for parents to follow at every practice or game:

1. Praise and celebrate your child's effort levels and overall sportsmanship above results such as winning.

2. *Please do not* coach from behind the chain-link fences.

3. *Please do not* yell at other coaches or their players.

4. *Please do not* interact with an umpire in a negative manner.

5. Stay away from the dugouts during the game. Make sure your player comes to practice or a game with enough fluids to stay hydrated.

6. Always try to have conversations after the practice or game about effort, not results. The car ride home is one of the best times to talk with your child.

7. Encourage your player with positivity. Point out the positive and be very specific. Try using these five words before every conversation regarding their performance, good or bad: I LOVE WATCHING YOU PLAY. Then talk about the specifics.

8. Cheer for the entire team, not just your child. Even applaud the other team if they display a great level of effort or acts of sportsmanship.

9. Enjoy the game! Baseball should be fun to play and watch. Remember, in the end, it is a game.

10. Let the coach do the coaching. I mentioned this earlier in the chapter. The coach is volunteering his or her time to help your player. Please be patient, kind, and respectful.

Triple Crown Tip: Try to put yourself in their shoes before criticizing. Asking your coach what you can do to help is always more productive than telling them what you think they should be doing.

Your child's success or lack of success in baseball does not always indicate what kind of parent you are. But having an athlete who tries their best and is coachable, respectful, a great teammate, mentally tough, and resilient *is* a direct reflection of your parenting.

Remember, regardless of what Tom Hanks said (*A League of Their Own*), there is crying in baseball. They're kids. Kids cry all the time. They cry when they get hurt. They cry when they make a mistake. They cry when they're embarrassed. But being kids, they'll stop crying in a minute, and they'll move on. Telling them to grow up, shake it off, or rub some dirt on it isn't going to help at that moment. It will only make matters worse. Just give them a second to collect themselves, and they'll bounce back. Kids are very resilient.

Also keep in mind that cursing shouldn't be your second language. Regardless of whether you think it's okay to swear in front of your kids, it's not okay to swear in front of other people's kids. Remember where you are. This isn't an R-rated movie. It's a ball park with kids and grandparents. We all can get over-excited when watching our children play sports. Be respectful to those around you and don't say or do things to embarrass your player.

One of my worst memories as a youth baseball player was seeing a very talented teammate's parent get angry at him for his performance during a Little League game. After the game, the parent picked the child up off the ground and slammed him against the fence in front of about a hundred people. Not only did this physically hurt the child, but it also embarrassed him beyond words. To this day, I will never forget that moment, and I'm sure my former teammate won't either. Please think twice about your actions before doing them, as they have a huge impact on the child.

Baseball can draw parents to emotional excess because it lets them do what normal parenting doesn't allow: cheer out loud for their child when they are under pressure and something's on the line. The great life lesson of baseball is that even the great players strike out often—three out of ten times—or make an error or baserunning mistake. The key to the game, as in life, is to experience failure, adapt, and learn to hit more than you miss. It is a joy to be able to participate in this life lesson because most of the time you won't be there. Really think about it . . . you can't show up at the SAT test to root for your child. After they strike out with a girl or a boy on their first date, you can't magically appear and show them in front of everyone that you support them no matter what happens. Wow, would that be awkward.

Excessive behavior can be embarrassing to your child and others. It teaches your child all the wrong lessons about sportsmanship, character, and respect. But even if you're not risking those outcomes, there is a challenge to finding the line between unconditional love and too much intensity. Even if you stop short of acting like the "over the top" parent, there's a finer line to walk here. You don't want to smother the experience for them with too much engagement. It's their game—just as it's their life.

In baseball, as in life, all the important things happen at home!

—Baseballisms

CHAPTER 3: COACH

During a season a few years back, my Little League team (ages ten to eleven) was struggling to make quick decisive decisions on defense. As a play would happen, we would be a few seconds late in reacting, failing to get that all-important last out to get us off the field. After a game in which we committed multiple errors on offense and defense, it really started to become obvious that my players were not yet mentally tough. If you have ever coached youth baseball, you know exactly what I'm referring to. One play goes badly, then another, it takes the air right out of them.

During our next practice, I decided to change some things up a bit. Before we started our routine, defensive work-up drills, I explained to every player if we didn't make the proper throw, they could expect physical conditioning to follow. This was not to punish them, but rather to condition their minds. As we progressed through the drills, the kids made mistakes.

After their mistakes, we did push-ups, jumping jacks, and running. After each exercise, the kids grew tired, but the lesson really started to sink in at that point. Each player started to try harder and maintain focus because as they became physically fatigued, I was attempting to train their minds to tell them they needed to perform better on each play to avoid future physical stress.

Since the beginning of time, the human body has been programmed to respond from a "fight or flight" survival mode. Millions of years ago, when flesh-eating dinosaurs chased us around the earth, we had two options: run or stand and fight. (If it was a Tyrannosaurus rex, I hope most took option number one!) Both options were designed to try to keep us alive! At many of my practices during the baseball season, I run drills that test this very response. I push the players to the brink of exhaustion and then ask them to react quickly to a mentally challenging situation. The majority struggle with it at first, but after a short time they become conditioned to react under stressful situations and show signs of improvement.

Triple Crown Tip: As a coach, be ready to sometimes change gears. This doesn't mean you should show up to practice every day with a plan and then throw it all out the window as soon as one thing goes wrong. Rather, it suggests you adapt to how your team is responding and adjust to their needs. This may happen in the middle of a practice or a game. A good coach can always follow the book. A great coach can think outside the box or diamond, being proactive and reactive when needed.

During my journey as a coach, I have been asked to visit other teams' practices, and when it comes to a practice plan, unfortunately I usually see the same thing time after time. When asked to help with a Little League (ages eleven and twelve) baseball team's practice a few years ago, the first thing I asked upon arriving was, "Hey, Coach, what's the plan today?"

The coach's response was this: "I thought we would let the kids start out by doing some fielding practice."

My response, with some doubt in my mind, especially as the kids hadn't even warmed up their bodies or arms yet, was "OK. Let's see what you got." I hoped things would improve as we progressed.

The coach sent all of his players to the nine designated spots on the field, with a couple of the players sharing a position. He then proceeded to do what most normal first-time youth baseball coaches do. He hit the ball to each position, one at a time, and asked them to make a play on the ball. This is a classic defensive-minded drill that has been used since the creation of baseball. Its effectiveness is minimal; however, as many of the players stand around and watch as the ball is hit somewhere else. Nonetheless, I continued to observe without comment.

After the coach spent twenty to thirty minutes giving the players minimal reps at each position, we moved into their batting practice. Again, I was thinking, "This will be the point where the pace picks up." I was taken aback as all of the players stayed in their positions while the coach threw twenty to thirty pitches to each batter. As the kids were called in one at a time to hit, the rest stood motionless for the next forty-five minutes. Some picked daisies in the outfield in between pitches.

Finally, after each player had batted, everybody huddled together as the coach encouraged the kids and told them they had a great practice. Meanwhile, in my head, I felt empty and couldn't help but think he had missed an opportunity to coach the players. After nearly ninety minutes of practice, they hadn't even broken a sweat or—worse—learned anything new fundamentally. Once the players had packed up their equipment and left the field, I approached the coach. The first question he asked me was, "So, how do you think practice went? Pretty good, right?"

I responded with, "Well, not so good." I then explained that it wasn't an attack on him as a person or as a volunteer coach. It was just that he lacked the experience and knowledge to set up a productive practice. But I was there to help in any way I could. At one point I had done the same thing and made a lot of mistakes during my first few years as a coach.

He was somewhat shocked to hear my response, as many newer coaches are. He then asked me, "What do you suggest I should do to make my practices better?" Here is the outline that I suggested:

SAMPLE PRACTICE

Throwing:

1. Start by having the players run or jog (ten to fifteen minutes). This starts the blood flow to all of their muscles. Performing any throwing before running and stretching is not recommended. (Our shoulder muscles consist of millions of tiny fibers. Each time we throw a baseball, we tear a few.)

2. Have the players form a circle and do stretches from toe to head (five minutes). The captain or co-captain stands in the center and leads the group.

3. Pair the kids up and start with short isolation throws twelve to fifteen feet apart (one knee). Oak throws—have them stand with feet planted in the ground and not move while throwing (five minutes).

4. Progressive throwing: move back a short-distance to full throws (five minutes).

5. Long toss: Move the players back three steps once both sides have thrown the baseball ten times. Throw all the way out to fifty yards (five minutes).

6. Long-toss elimination: At this distance, anyone who drops a baseball in the air or makes a bad throw runs to a designated area and then back to their equipment for a two- to three-minute break. The last pair to not drop the ball or make a bad throw is exempt from running.

7. 20-for-20 drill: Split the team evenly and place them at first and second base. This drill is a basic throwing-and-catching drill that gives the players high reps between a variety of players. One player throws from his base to the other base. As the other player catches the ball, he yells "One!" Then when that player throws it back to the base the baseball came from, the next player catches it cleanly and yells "Two!" If at any time a player fails to catch a throw or deliver a throw on target, the entire group must start over from the beginning. The goal is to get from zero

to twenty in the least number of throws. This is a great team unity drill. It requires the whole team to pay attention and concentrate while making accurate throws.

Fielding:

1. Bare-hand ground-ball drill: Pair up players and have them take their gloves off, throwing ground balls back and forth from fifteen to twenty feet away, fielding every ball in front with their bare hands. This helps players follow the baseball all the way into their hands to make sure they field it cleanly. If everyone does well with their bare hands, then the team is allowed to put their gloves on and work the same drill, moving back twenty more feet.

2. Crisscross ground ball and fly ball drill: Split the team into two even groups. One group will line up behind the first person at the second base and shortstop positions. A coach and assistant will hit ground balls and infield fly balls from behind the first base and third base infield foul lines. This drill allows a player to have multiple reps from each side of the infield diamond, fielding baseballs on the ground and in the air. Coaches and players need to make sure they don't come forward on a ball hit short, as they will run the risk of being hit in the crossfire of another ground ball. This helps players to keep their eyes in front and to always be on high alert while the ball is in play.

Hitting:

For the hitting portion of the practice, I showed the coach what I like to call my "snake batting practice" (snake BP). His team at the time had eleven players, which worked out great because the ideal number of players for this drill is ten to thirteen. A coach with a full bucket of balls pitches from the front of the pitcher's mound. (If you are pitching to kids over ten years of age, I suggest you use an L-screen protective fence.) Another empty bucket is put at the edge of the grass directly behind second base to collect any balls that the batters hit into the outfield. A tee with Wiffle balls is set up just to the right of the third base dugout, closest to left field. This will be the position prior to going into the dugout and being the on-deck batter. A player is put into position for left field, center field, right field, first base, second base, shortstop, and third base, with one player at the outfield bucket. There is no catcher.

There are also two protector positions: one in front of the outfield bucket, to protect the player fielding incoming balls who may have his or her back turned, and one in foul territory, protecting the player hitting off the tee. All players get twelve to fifteen pitches to hit and then rotate in a snake formation from outfield to infield, onto the tee, then in to bat. When the coach says to rotate, all players in the corresponding areas make sure the baseballs are collected and returned to the coach's bucket. The setup can be flipped to run from either dugout.

I know some of you seasoned coaches are asking, "Why do the batters get only twelve to fifteen pitches?" The answer is simple: *efficiency*. DO NOT waste the players' practice time. The key is to give each player an adequate number of swings and then get them back out of there while having another batter with a helmet ready to jump in.

To be as efficient as possible you should come prepared with a plan. (I will mention this at least half a dozen times during this book.) As a coach, I recommend you spend thirty minutes the day before formulating a plan for practices and games. For example, the plan could include working on fundamentals, identifying what you did wrong at the last game and how to fix it, and conditioning. Most coaches are volunteers, so I know this can be a daunting task if you have a full-time job and family, but the plan works best if you prepare it before practice begins. Try to never schedule a practice that you're not prepared for ahead of time—even if "prepared" means you have a few bullet points written down in your smartphone that you must cover. If you're not prepared, think about cancelling it or rescheduling! One of the most important reasons to have a plan is to show the players, and their parents, that you are organized and care about leading them.

A plan helps to keep the pace of practice going, which, more times than not, keeps your players moving and challenges them both physically and mentally. If you don't have a plan and are disorganized, both players and parents may become complacent and start to question what you are trying to have them accomplish as a team. Without a plan, it can become easy for someone to point the finger at the coach if something goes wrong.

Having a plan goes hand in hand with setting your expectations at the beginning of the season. Once you set your expectations for both parents and players, put them in writing. Then you can go back and hold yourself, the players, and the parents accountable for meeting the list of agreed upon expectations.

Triple Crown Tip: I suggest every coach put together a player and parent expectation agreement. The agreement should include all of your expectations for the upcoming season. For example, what your expectations are for practice, games, and tournaments. It should also include a list of acceptable behavior and communication requirements. These are just few things that need to be included. In most leagues they may already have this available to coaches. Just make sure to print a copy off, review it with your players and parents, and then have them sign it. Keep it in the team binder so you can go back and reference it at any time.

On the flip side, it's hopefully an expectation of most parents that their child's coach be prepared at every practice and game.

Coaches who can outline plays on a blackboard are a dime a dozen. The ones who win get inside their players and motivate.

—Vince Lombardi

MOTIVATION

We all know it can be extremely difficult for coaches to get players to stay focused and work hard through an entire season. Yet player motivation can have a huge effect on your success. If you can effectively motivate your players, they usually learn much faster, win more games, learn useful life lessons, improve skills at a faster rate, have more fun in the process, and become better players and people because of it.

To help you motivate your players and keep them more focused than ever before, I have put together a guide for player motivation. Several of these ideas came from exceptional coaches that I have come across over the years. Others express my personal beliefs on how to motivate players in youth baseball.

Hopefully you will find this information valuable when things get difficult and your players start to lose focus. Trust me, no matter how good of a coach you are, you will probably hit a wall at some point. We all do. I have listed many motivational techniques for you to utilize as you see fit.

The Answer Depends on Your Question

Before I get started, you must realize that no single answer exists for all of your questions on how to motivate every player you coach. I continue to learn every year. Your techniques will mostly depend on the age level of your players (tee-ball to high school), your years of coaching experience, your individual style, the resources at your disposal, and the types of players you have.

For example, a rookie coach (tee-ball) may need to use different techniques than a twenty-five-year seasoned veteran (high school or college) with a proven track record and an established program. A youth coach working with five-to-seven-year-olds may simply use the one-to-three count technique, where you slowly count to three in a stern voice, to maintain attention and motivate younger players. But a high school coach would likely not use the same technique.

Keep in mind that each player can respond differently to motivational tactics. It usually boils down to what makes them tick. One player might be motivated by having playing time during a game, while another player might just want to feel part of the team. Some players respond to adversity; some don't. It's important not to treat them all the same, because they are not!

From what I have experienced, what works for one coach might not work for another. Many of the things I have learned about coaching are lessons learned from other coaches. I held onto the things that worked best for me and let go of those that didn't fit my personality or style. All of this relates to learning, applying, and growing from the success or failure. For example, I would learn something new from another coach and then use it during a practice or game. Then if it worked well for me, I would use it again. If not, I wouldn't.

That's why I put together such a huge list of techniques and tips that have worked for me—so you can quickly and easily mold your own formula to motivate players. I will also address specific situations and age levels to make this list more useful for everyone.

10 *Triple Crown* Motivational Techniques

We're starting with the techniques that I feel are most effective. Again, it depends on your situation, but these techniques have been effective for me personally. After reading these techniques, you might have everything you need, but I will still offer you more tips as well. Since this is my ultimate guide to motivation, I'm offering you all kinds of information to choose from. Remember, use what fits, and disregard what doesn't.

Technique #1—Identify What Motivates Each Player

Identifying what motivates your players should go a long way in your overall success. I feel that every good coach must do two things: teach and motivate! Few coaches tend to devote the time or energy needed to understand how to motivate others. Yet motivating players can be the difference between a subpar season and a championship-caliber season. Hard work and motivation can dramatically improve players' overall skills and conditioning, improve execution, accelerate the learning process, and improve everything a team needs to be more successful. Simply recognizing and considering the importance of what motivates each individual can make the difference in how hard your players work during a season. As an example, at the beginning of each season I like to ask each player these three questions: What do you like about the game of baseball? Can you describe to me a moment when you had fun playing the game of baseball? What motivates you to keep playing each year? I then use the answers they give me to identify what motivates them. My goal is that if I can touch their heart, their head will follow. Meaning that if I can pinpoint what motivates them, they will then be open and willing to learn.

Build Relationships

One of my favorite ways to motivate players is to show that I care about them outside of baseball. You can do this by taking a sincere interest in what they do outside of youth baseball. For example, during some of the downtime before or after practices, ask them what they do during their free time. Do you play video games? Do you like to watch movies? What's your favorite food? These are simple questions that don't take up a lot of time. Get to know them. Support them. Show a genuine interest. This will show them that you really care about them and will help you build a better relationship. Once they believe you truly care, they will go to war for you.

In my mind, there is no better feeling than to see a player I coached in the past, and they still call me coach, many years later. It also gives me great pleasure to see them playing baseball at the high school level or beyond. This tells me that I earned their respect as a coach and as a friend. It also tells me that they had fun and still enjoy playing the game. To me those things are priceless.

What do you know about your players? What makes them tick? Do you know how to deal with age differences? You can't coach eight-year-olds as though they are high school players, and vice versa.

Here is a thought for you to ponder: almost everyone is motivated by the same thing—success. However, the differences in individual people lead to varying definitions of success. In baseball, it can be playing time, scoring a lot of runs, just making the team, winning, or impressing a family member or girlfriend. It's the coach's role to find out what motivates each of their players. It will definitely be different for different people.

The way to figure this out is by spending time trying to learn your players' motivations. Most coaches ask that their players dedicate time outside of practice to do the necessary things to improve. As a coach, you must understand that players are motivated by both on- and off-the-diamond issues. Learning what those things are can maximize your return.

Technique #2—Inspire Your Players by Teaching Them

To coach is to teach. What is the priority and overall concern of a teacher? It's the constant progression of their students, not wins and losses or stats. This is a very simple yet profound concept that coaches should attempt to fully embrace. When you as the coach treat each player as unique individuals, the players—and the team overall—can show tremendous improvement.

When you show and demonstrate to the players that you care about them as individuals and as a team (this can be done with words and/or a pat on the back), they will care about what you have to say (you've gained influence), and the door is open to truly effective teaching and learning. You can teach or coach your rear end off, and be absolutely correct on all the information you give out, but if the player isn't with you, it could be an uphill battle.

The reality that some miss is that during the games, players tend to do exactly what they do or see in practice. We do this from the time we are born till the day we die. For those of you who have already coached, I'm sure the saying, "You practice like you play" is all too familiar. But how many coaches actually live by this saying? Please don't fool yourself. A spirited pre-game speech will not always light a fire that lasts the entire game or practice. This is not the answer. The easiest way to motivate your players is to teach them what you know. After they notice their own improvement ("aha" moment), they will have even greater motivation.

Again, it is important to treat your players like they are unique individuals, because they are. Each one of them is an individual with different desires, needs, and experience. Strive to teach them every day. Help them and challenge them to improve. Inspire each player to want to learn more. Make sure they see that they are improving, and point out the results. Success breeds success. Building off of the success can create positive experiences. If you feel like you've hit a wall, seek help from an experienced coach. The use of this simple tool alone can make you more successful than you ever thought possible. *Do not* be afraid to ask for help!

Technique #3—Motivate Through Example and Explanation

Over the past seventeen years, I have been employed in the industrial sales field, and I have found several ways to incorporate what I've learned from sales into my everyday life and coaching. A good teacher—and salesperson, for that matter—can typically explain the "why." A coach often needs to put his or her sales hat on to ensure that players believe. You have to get them to buy into what you're coaching them. You have to sell it! Here is an example. During your next practice get out on the field and show your kids how to physically perform the drill. Pick up your glove and field a ground ball alongside your players. Grab a bat during batting practice and show them how to perform a proper swing. One of my favorites is to run with your players at the end of practice. All of these actions can help sell it to your players.

Players often don't understand why they are asked to do a certain drill, and they lose motivation. This is why I am asking you to explain why the fundamental drills are important and what they are designed to do. Don't assume the players already know, because I promise that not all do. One of the best ways to find out what they know is by asking questions. In asking questions to a player or team, you give them an opportunity and a voice.

Explaining why is also a proven psychological trigger that causes people to take a certain action. At a psychological level, humans want to know why they are doing something. Let's take not hustling on every play as an example. If your players don't understand the reason you want them to hustle, they will *not* give 100 percent! If you are asking them to give 100 percent, you need to explain the reason why. Why are you asking them to hustle on every play? The answer is simple: you never know when the ball will be hit to you, so it is important to be prepared for it every time, so that when it is actually hit to you, you are ready. Teach them why they're supposed to run hard to first base on every ground ball hit in the infield. Teach them why they should always hustle and how it can affect their team. The more your players understand, the more they will buy into it and perform at a higher level!

Triple Crown Tip: Don't slow your practice to a crawl, but work the explanations in at times when players might not like what you're having them do. Try this out and see how it works. You will be surprised at how effective it really is!

Technique #4—Encourage Continual Improvement and Growth the Entire Season

As I mentioned earlier, one of the best motivational tools of all can be for athletes to see and feel that they are continually improving. The beginning of the season is always very productive because it's brand new and fresh, and players feel like they are quickly getting better each day. As the season moves on, players may feel that they are no longer showing improvement. This makes it really tough for them to focus and to keep working hard. Kids are motivated by progress and growth, so offering constant feedback on their efforts and performance is very important—especially for the kids who don't play very much.

It can be difficult to motivate the players who are often substitutes. I try to have one practice each week in which the head coach works only with the substitutes, and my assistant coaches work with the starters; but never put up a wall or divide the players just based on their skill levels. In other words, don't show favoritism toward one group or the other, and make it apparent to every player that each week positions can be won or lost. Strive to have each individual feel that they have been successful at some point in the practice. This doesn't mean they made the ESPN Top 10 Play, were the fastest runner during a sprint drill, or made the best hit during BP, but it might mean they arrived at practice first or remembered to bring an extra glove to help out a teammate who forgot his or hers. There are many ways to ensure that your players feel successful. Get creative!

Set Goals

Players need both short-term and long-term goals. Both need to be touched on regularly. Short term might be winning the team's first game, while long term could be winning your respective league. The key is to set obtainable goals and also provide frequent feedback.

I believe goals in life and baseball are very important, and when done properly, they can be extremely effective. But you need to be careful with this as well. Be sure that the goals do not set your players up for failure (i.e., winning every game, scoring the most runs, allowing the least number of runs).

The key here is not to overdo it with too many goals; choose realistic goals that mean something. Players and teams need goals so they know what to focus on and shoot for, but the key is the type of goals you choose.

I'm a firm believer that you should *not* set goals related to prestigious statistics, such as having the most hits and even winning games. Players already want those things without setting any goals. Additionally, it can give players the wrong idea. By wrong, I mean that the individual statistics may spoil what you're trying to accomplish as a team.

Conversely, if you set team goals for important aspects of the game, you should see huge success! (i.e., on-base percentage, sacrifice bunts, defensive assists) Make sure you don't forget to provide frequent feedback on their status, rewarding or praising players for achieving their goals.

Youth athletes need to have a clear definition of what they are expected to achieve. Goals should also be individualized for each player. This can be difficult to do at times because people tend not to be motivated by goals they view as either too easy or too difficult.

> *If you've got a dozen pitchers, you need to speak twelve different languages.*
>
> —Michael Lewis, *Moneyball*

Technique #5—Measure Player Performance

Measuring performance may sound like the same thing as setting goals, but it's not the same thing. Simply show the right statistics, and your players will boost their performance. You'll be surprised how effective this can be. Sharing the numbers in practice and talking about them helps make players more aware of how they are performing on the diamond. The key is to share the data; don't hide it. Simply sharing the data improves performance and creates passive motivation. There are so many things you can measure: team statistics, individual statistics, player sacrifices, and so on. There are way too many options to mention them all. Please don't feel like you have to go out and build a massive Excel spreadsheet and print it out for your whole team to read. It can be as simple as showing them your home book once a week after a game.

All you need to do is think about what's *important* to you and your team. Then think about what you can measure to determine if you're doing a good job in that area. You don't think you can measure everything that's important to you? You'd be surprised what you can measure when you put some serious thought into it.

Technique #6— Be Organized, Creative, and Confident

A disorganized and unbalanced training session or practice can hinder players from giving their best. Plan ahead and gear up toward the individual team's needs. Remember, variety is the spice of life! Your practices and conditioning should always be both mentally and physically stimulating, yet fun.

As a coach, make sure that your practices are constantly evolving as the season progresses. In other words, change up your drills and routines to ensure there is an element of challenge and growth at all times. For example, do more conditioning at the beginning of your practice, instead of at the end, and then do something fun at the end, as opposed to always ending with base running or sprints. Keep the players on their toes and try not follow the same pattern.

Players need to feel confident that their coach knows what he or she is talking about. If you are unsure of a certain element of the game, study the fundamentals, ask questions to gain knowledge, learn, and then coach with confidence. Without the players' confidence, how can a coach even begin to motivate? A confident coach instills confidence in their players.

Are you starting to see how so many of the tools are closely related? Here is another similar tool that I use:

Technique #7—Celebrate the Small Accomplishments, Both Team and Individual

Instead of concentrating on winning, put players in a situation in which they can experience a different type of success. For example, if you work on a fielding drill, you can track their progress and show their improvement in fielding percentages during a game. Celebrate these small accomplishments! You can also measure things like errors and putouts, acknowledging improvement in those areas. Show them how they are improving! Don't just tell them.

As the season progresses, constantly remind them of how much they have improved. Remind them of how they were batting a few weeks ago. Remind them of how much their fielding has improved since the very first practice. Remind them of how much their baserunning and pitching has progressed since the first game. Be specific.

Youth players want to be successful and have a lot of fun. But unfortunately, not everyone can win. That's why it's important for coaches to find other ways for players to obtain success.

For example, a few times I like to use praise is when a player or players do the following:

1. Finish a tough drill
2. Meet a specific goal
3. Achieve accurate throws
4. Make consecutive throws without dropping a ball
5. Learn a new skill
6. Learn a new defensive position
7. Break a bad habit
8. Demonstrate great teamwork

Don't let a losing season bring you or your team down. I know it can be hard, but just because you lost every game doesn't mean the season was *not* a success! If your players improved, had some fun, and learned life lessons (i.e., overcame adversity during a tough at bat, helped a player when they were hurt, showed sportsmanship for the other team, respected the umpires), then it was most certainly a success! Celebrate those accomplishments. That's really what coaching and baseball are all about.

Reward Hard Work, and Give Positive Reinforcement

Just as happens in life, coaches get exactly what they give. I believe it's that simple, really. That's why when a coach is committed to working hard and giving max effort, that's what he or she often gets in return. This is a very important topic to understand.

So what is positive reinforcement in youth baseball? Positive reinforcement is giving a player a reward immediately following a behavior to encourage that player to focus on doing the right thing and repeating that behavior. If a player is rewarded for a great throw in a drill, they will want to do that action again because they gain approval for it. When the other players see that this behavior gets rewarded, they will also try to copy the behavior because they want a reward too. An example of a reward would be to lessen how much that player is required to run during a conditioning drill. It's not that you give them an "act lazy card" and they get to skip the entire drill. It's a small reward for maintaining concentration on the task at hand.

When players do things the right way, or do them well, it is necessary that you reward them for their actions. This could be a simple, "Great job," but a more tangible reward, as mentioned earlier, works even better. Why does positive reinforcement work? Positive reinforcement is successful with players because it focuses on the positive stuff rather than on the negative events that occur. Positive reinforcement also gives players psychological satisfaction. Give specific praise, and give a lot of it.

Types of Rewards and Reinforcement

There are many ways to reward players and offer positive reinforcement. For example, you can and should give frequent verbal reinforcement in practices and in games. Players love to hear compliments, it can really grab their attention and motivates.

Occasionally, for max effort, praise players in front of the entire team. Public praise is often well received, and players will work hard to earn such praise. I suggest using a technique I have used over the years. Praise in public, and criticize behind closed doors. You can do this by addressing the team as a unit, waiting to hold your individual conversations with players during a break, before or after practices, and so on. Here are a few reward ideas to consider:

1. Giving specific verbal encouragement
2. Momentarily pausing practice to highlight a positive behavior
3. Giving out oranges during a break
4. Going out for pizza or ice cream after practice
5. Playing Wiffle ball the last half of practice
6. Going to a high school, legion, or college game instead of having practice
7. Giving more playing time in a desired position
8. Letting a player hit first during batting practice or even during the next game

The bottom line is to reward them when they play hard or when something positive stems from their hard work and preparation.

To keep players motivated, the frequency in which you offer feedback is paramount. Positive reinforcement works best when it isn't a once-in-a-while thing; the more it occurs, the more effective it is. If most of your focus is on the negative, it will eat away at your team's morale.

Be Specific

When you praise a player at any level of youth baseball, it is best to be specific with your choice of words. Obviously saying something like "great job" or "nice hit" is better than nothing, but being specific helps to promote the positive action or behavior you want. The players will also feel like you are paying attention to what they do if you are specific with your praise.

A great example would be, "Good job stopping that hard-hit ground ball from reaching the outfield," instead of "Nice stop, Jimmy." And, "Way to keep your glove down on that bad hop," is better than, "Nice work." Let them know exactly what you want. Make sure to explain in detail what you want in a way that communicates to a player who isn't playing up to your expectation.

Reduce Negative Feedback

Screaming at a player from the dugout can cause embarrassment, and when it is done too often, it can damage the player's confidence and motivation. How can you correct errors in a group setting using a positive approach?

One method I use is to substitute the player after an error during a timeout and provide feedback in the dugout, not in a huddle on the mound. I know that can be difficult to do, so you can also save feedback for after the game, if need be. Timing and tone is the key.

I feel most coaches jump in too fast and correct. If you give your player time, you'll often find they correct the error on their own. With that being said, at times correction may be necessary, and when it is, try to avoid too much negative feedback. Sometimes you just need to let the small things go. I struggled with this early on as a coach and slowly improved with experience.

Technique #8—Make It Fun and Competitive

Human beings are generally motivated by things they enjoy, so the goal is to have *fun*, especially with youth players! As the players get older, adding a competitive aspect to practice can really push the players to work even harder, even passing points they never thought were possible.

Let's face it. Do you really think players will be motivated to work hard if they know that the drills will be monotonous and super hard and that they'll be yelled at by someone acting as a drill sergeant? Of course not! You may see an initial reaction from a player, but in the long run that may hinder your player-coach relationships. If you are a newer coach, please avoid this path. I found out the hard way my first couple of years coaching. It can be twice as hard to build the rapport back up with your players after acting in this manner.

Players need to work hard, but *if* they are having fun at practice or game, you will get the best out of them. Learn to laugh with them, even if it's at your own expense. Coaches that make mistakes, then own up to it, earn the respect of their players. Don't be afraid to admit you're wrong. To make practice fun, be sure to have fun yourself. Smile and enjoy the process.

Most importantly, youth players, who are in fact kids, enjoy succeeding. So be sure to run drills and put kids in situations where they can be successful. Set them up for success, not failure.

You can make almost any ordinary drill fun. Just use your imagination. Here are a few examples that I like to use:

1. Turn a drill into a competitive game. Nothing says *fun* like a game. You can turn a simple bunting drill into a game by using chalked circles (I have found that inverted athletic marking paint works the best, as it will wear off after being sprayed on grass or dirt) to see who can place the ball best. If you miss the circle, you're out. The player with the best bunt wins.

2. You can incorporate other sports, such as football and baseball, to come up with new drills. Have your catcher throw a football from home to second base to increase arm strength and accuracy. I know that sounds weird, but give it a try and see the reaction on your catcher's face when it helps increase their accuracy.

3. Offering points will make any drill enjoyable. Allow players to earn redeemable points for paying attention, properly executing a drill, helping out a teammate, or whatever you choose. Points can get players rewards that range from a Gatorade to fewer sprints.

4. Keep kids moving at all times, with none standing in lines waiting for more than thirty seconds before the next movement. A fun drill to improve the kids' hand-eye coordination is what I call the "hot circle." Form a circle with all of your players. Then hand a player one baseball and have them underhand toss it to the player to their right. Each player continues to toss the baseball around the circle counterclockwise while keeping their feet stationary. Once the players go around the circle several times, stop them and add another baseball. You can add more baseballs or yell out, "Reverse," and have them toss each ball the opposite direction. The object is to not let a ball hit the ground and keep them all focused and moving at the same time. This is a fun drill that all my players have enjoyed.

5. Use multifaceted drills that are stimulating both mentally and physically. For example, I use a drill that I picked up from a coach several years ago called "ten on and ten off." Before performing this drill, make sure all your players know the numbered positions for each defensive spot. This is how it works. Line all your players up along the backstop and have them face out toward the pitcher's mound. Go down the line of players and assign a number from one to nine (the nine positions on the baseball field). After you assign each player a number, you yell, "Go!" The coach or assistant then counts ten seconds. Every player must be at the assigned position before the coach reaches ten. This will require each player to sprint in

order to make it in time. After every player reaches the designated position, the coach then yells, "Go!" again and counts backward from ten down to zero. All players must sprint back to the same spot against the backstop. As the coach, you can have a lot of fun with this drill. I usually start by sending the players to the positions they generally play at. This will help them get better by knowing where to be on defense during different situations. It also helps the players memorize each number, so they will understand what they are looking at when they see it on a batting lineup or box score. After you have built up some rapport with your team, later in the season, try this variation: Give all of your players the number nine (right field), except for one. Give that one player number seven (left field). When they all get to the two positions, it's funny to see the looks on their faces. One player will be in left field all alone, and the rest of your team will be in right field. Once I bring the players back to the backstop, I usually ask the player that was in left field if he or she forgot to wear deodorant. Most of the kids will laugh, but I will let you use your discretion on whether or not to use that variation.

Triple Crown Tip: At the beginning of a season, it is important to build up arm strength to prevent injuries. As mentioned earlier, set up a long toss from home plate to centerfield. In centerfield, make a large circle with ten baseballs. Each player gets two throws from home plate to try to get their ball into the circle in centerfield. This will make it competitive for the players and will help with arm strength and accuracy of longer-distance throws. (Please make sure your players' arms are good and warm before attempting these throws.)

With a little planning and imagination, you can come up with ways to make almost all of your drills competitive but fun. Just keep in mind that comparisons between teammates can make some players feel badly and can spur rivalries between teammates. For example, don't set up a drill where a smaller player with less arm strength is matched up against a teammate twice their size that can throw a baseball from home to the centerfield fence with ease. In short, it can squash a player's motivation if not handled correctly.

In addition, competition can hinder *new* skill development. When players are learning a brand-new skill, you should remove all competition and give them as many reps as possible. You certainly don't want to overdo it when adding competition to drills.

Here are a few more ideas for how to add competition to drills and practice:

1. Competitive live scrimmages: Two balls and two strikes as the starting count on all batters. This will keep the pace of your practice moving while adding a competitive edge.

2. Competitive base-running drills: reward the winner or make the loser run.

3. Four-on-four competitive fielding drills: the group with the least amount of errors wins.

4. Competitive pitching: the most strikes in ten pitches wins.

5. Relay-throwing drill: the winner gets an extra five-minute break.

6. King-of-the-hill drill (i.e., organized fielding drill): all teammates must bow to the winner on the mound.

These are just a few examples of the ideas I use. There are so many more. I encourage you to use whatever baseball knowledge you have and make up your own.

Technique #9—Motivate by Forming Habits

Playing hard should not be something you save for the fifth inning or the end of a game. Playing hard should be a habit that you push your players to do *all the time*. Play every play like it's the last play of a championship game! The key is to get in the habit of playing hard no matter what the situation is. Players should go hard in practice, in each drill, and in every minute of the game, no matter what. Form the habit. Of course, that's easier said than done. But the tools I have provided should help you, and it's something a coach should always strive for.

You can't always inspire a player or team with a great speech. That type of thing only works for so long and eventually wears out. Players will become numb to the pre-game speeches and motivational talks. When it comes to putting the finished product on the field, or shall I say, playing the game, motivation must come from within them. Look at it this way: The players are on the field playing the game, not the coaches.

They will have the biggest impact on the outcome of a game, not *you*.

The key here is for players to develop the habit of giving 100 percent. If they give 100 percent in practice, they will give 100 percent in a game. They won't know how to play any other way. This is the *only* way to maintain intensity throughout the entire season. Without good habits, you're bound to have major inconsistencies and a lot of ups and downs.

You know how people with twenty-five New Year's resolutions barely even get to see one of them through to the end? Don't try to be perfect at everything. Coach your players to work on one habit at a time to the best of their ability. As they master each habit, like showing up ten minutes early to practice or staying after to work on an in which area they are struggling, you will eventually build a complete toolbox of good habits they can carry with them forever. But it doesn't happen in one night; it takes patience and due diligence. It took Cal Ripken lots of time and patience to break Lou Gehrig's consecutive games played record, but he did it.

Technique #10—Promote Teamwork

Generally, people are more apt to work hard for a team than for themselves. In business, the most successful organizations seem to bring one overriding purpose to the forefront, and the purpose is kept as a focal point for everyone involved. What is your team's collective purpose? Is it teamwork? Do some serious thinking to determine your team's collective purpose.

Consider emphasizing teamwork in your practices and games. Remind players they are stronger as a unit than as individuals. Give them some examples. Tell them a reference story. Stories are a powerful way to persuade and teach players important concepts. For instance, one year I had a team that was struggling to come together as a team. Many of the players only cared about the individual plays they made on defense or what they did during an at bat.

So after struggling through the first couple of practices and games, I finally came to the realization that the team had no real collective purpose. We had no idea what we were trying to accomplish as a team because too many were worrying about themselves. At the next practice we worked on some fielding drills. During those drills, I asked my shortstop after he fielded a ground ball to run the ball all the way to first and attempt to get the runner out on his own. He and the rest of his teammates looked at me with stunned faces. No matter how good of a player my shortstop was as an individual, there was no way he was going to be able to get the runner out on his own. I did this with several other drills during that practice. After the practice came to an end we huddled together as a team and I asked them all why they thought I had them do those drills. All of them responded with the same answer, "No one player is bigger than the game, and we all need our teammates to be successful."

Are your players a close group? Do they respect each other? What can you do to improve their relationships? You'll find that the hardest-working teams are often good friends, respect each other, believe in teamwork, and have camaraderie. Teams like this win championships, work hard, play for each other, and usually achieve the highest success.

Create Team Unity

If players like and respect each of their teammates, they will play hard for them. They will usually feel an obligation to make a play so as not to let their teammates down.

Here are a few techniques I use to improve team unity:

High fives: Instruct the leaders on your team to get in the habit of giving lots of high fives. Have you noticed how many times MLB players give out high fives and hugs on the field or in the dugout during a game? This is a proven technique that can bring an upbeat attitude to the game, improve players' confidence, and improve unity.

Attend a fun event as a team—other baseball games, an arcade, or a water park. Having fun as a team doing something off the field can help build team chemistry. In addition, teach your players commitment, particularly commitment to the team and to themselves. Many young athletes have never committed to anything in their lives. To obtain their commitment, you must do at least three things. First, explain what commitment means and discuss it with the group. Example: "Commitment is a promise to focus completely at practice." Second, ask for their commitment. This will often take the form of a verbal agreement. Third, be explicit in explaining the benefits of committing to the team.

Learning to commit to one thing will help them learn to commit to other things, such as schoolwork, relationships, staying fit, and social causes. Struggling to maintain a commitment with teammates will strengthen their bonds. Committed players learn to support each other the way they in turn receive support from others.

When you're part of a team, you stand up for your teammates. Your loyalty is to them. You protect them through good and bad, because they'd do the same for you.

—Yogi Berra

10 *Triple Crown* Tips to Coaching Success

Tip #1—Set the Tone with Discipline Early

A simple way I establish control is to set a precedent on the first day of practice. Establishing your expectations from the very beginning is the best way to not only establish your role within the team, but also to let your players know that you're serious.

Triple Crown Tip: As your first practice starts and players are moving about the field, touch the top of your hat and call them to the pitcher's mound. If they don't sprint hard to you, send them back to where they came from. After they've made it back, touch the top of your hat again and call them to you again. This time, all of your players will enthusiastically sprint to you. More importantly, you'll have their full attention for the rest of the year. This is a great time to explain to them what your expectations are. Players should be hustling at all times while on the baseball field. If your team is younger (i.e., tee-ball, machine pitch, coach pitch) the "count 1...2...3... method" can be used to give them more time to react and to gain their attention.

Tip #2—Keep the Lines of Communication Open

Constantly have your lines of communications open. Encourage your players and parents to talk to you often. Some will, some won't, and some might do both, depending on the situation. It is something that has to be constantly reinforced by you, the coach. A lot of the time it is just asking them questions and listening. If they reach out to you, be there for them and make it a priority to respond. At times, I believe we all struggle with this, but slowing down and doing those two important things can be beneficial.

Tip #3—Playing Time Is Earned, Not Given

When a player's attention wanes, his attitude is not so great, or his effort is less than 100 percent, he should be reminded that playing time is earned, not given. *Do not* allow players to participate in practice if they are constantly misbehaving. The reward for good behavior should be participation in practice, not just in games. Sometimes kids behave poorly simply to get attention. With youth players, it is important to reward the behavior you want, and address the behavior you don't want.

Tip #4—Avoid Team Punishment

I used to believe in team rewards and team penalties. If one player was late, everyone would run. The purpose was to try to make each player responsible to the others. Theoretically, the slackers will be raised by the achievers. Unfortunately, it doesn't always work that way. The negative influences always win out over the positive ones. What happened was the responsible players developed animosity toward the irresponsible ones. It also removed the incentive for them to do the right thing—"Why should I be on time when I have to run anyway?"—and created anger toward me as the coach for punishing them even when they did the right thing. I believe that even in a team setting, players have to be held accountable individually for their own actions. That helps the other players focus on what they believe is important.

Tip #5—Have a Change of Face

Players can get bored with the same old faces! Try bringing in new coaches with fresh and different ideas, perhaps even on a short-term basis. Invite a former player from the area who went on to play college baseball, minor leagues, or even MLB. I strive to do this at least once a year. It gives the players something to look forward to and a chance to meet someone they admire or look up to. Plus it helps break up the monotony of everyday practice.

Tip #6—Communicate Each Player's Role

Players need to know their roles. Let every athlete on your team know exactly what they can contribute to the group. Even if it means explaining the value of a good right fielder or the importance of batting in the number nine position.

Although it is easy to establish the roles of the more gifted athletes, it is much more challenging to connect with the athletes who are less gifted or less socially engaging. When a coach can bring the less skilled athletes into the fold, however, he or she achieves a far more meaningful satisfaction and success.

Tip #7—Maintain Consistency and Enthusiasm

Young players are often heard to say, "I hope the coach is in a good mood today." This indicates that the mood of the coach greatly affects the extent to which young people enjoy the sport.

The environment that you build, including what you say and how you say it, should be consistent, caring, and enthusiastic. Your behavior toward all young people, regardless of their ability, should be the same. A team is generally as consistent and enthusiastic as their coach.

Tip #8—Sometimes You Have to Talk About the Past to Improve the Future

If you've had hardworking, successful players in the past, talk about them. Tell their stories, both good and bad. Let your players learn from others before them. All good coaches do the same exact thing. Hearing these stories about players that the kids probably look up to will encourage and inspire them. ("If Jimmy played so hard and was one of the most successful players ever, maybe I should work hard too.") It also adds a little social proof that your coaching techniques work. I like to refer to this as a "reference story." (If you haven't noticed, I used a few in the first two chapters.)

Tip #9—Players in Leadership Roles Should Lead by Example

Choose leaders on your team who are hard-working and have a strong inner drive. Encourage them to lead by example with their actions. This is important because other players will follow them. Be sure to have a team captain or two co-captains. Assign responsibilities or roles to your leaders at practice, and ensure that they lead by example during games.

Tip #10—Slow Down, Speed Up, Keep Moving, Don't Stop!

To motivate kids, always try to keep your practice moving! *Do not* spend a lot of time on any one aspect of the game. Be short and sweet. For example, spend five to ten minutes on warm-up stretches and running, and ten minutes on throwing. If they are not progressing very quickly on a certain skill, then move on. Don't dwell on things for too long. Remember, most of the things you practice require a developmental process and usually do not have instantaneous results.

Keep things new. If things begin to slow, you can insert yourself into some drills with your players. Players like coaches who sweat alongside them, and will take it as a challenge to work harder to beat you.

It's tricky for new coaches to know how to organize a practice— when to give breaks, or when to use certain drills and for how long. But a good structure can break up the monotony, save time, and keep things flowing smoothly. Write down an organized list of items you need to accomplish at practice. Prioritize them one through five. If you don't get to number five by the end of your practice, make that your number-one priority at the next one.

One of the things I suggest is having a goal to stick to your scheduled practice plan. As hard as it may be at times, *do not* go past your scheduled time. If the kids find you doing that, they will start to pace themselves. As the season progresses, consider cutting back practice time. You don't want to deplete their legs on the practice field. Also, you will gain the respect of the parents who need to pick their children up on time.

Motivating Youth Players

To summarize, motivating youth players can be hard and easy at the same time. Younger players are usually less complicated than older players who are motivated by other things. Generally the younger players just want to *have fun* and enjoy playing the game. That is clearly one of their biggest motivational factors. But keep in mind that having a delicious treat (i.e., donuts, cookies, or cupcakes) after a game or practice works pretty good too! Again, there isn't one true right answer.

I hope the techniques and tips you just read will help aid your coaching efforts in the future.

CONCLUSION

This book has been full of ideas and suggestions about how to make youth baseball a positive experience for your children. Most parents want their player to come out of a youth baseball experience feeling like a winner, with self-confidence and a healthy attitude about sports. But how do you define winning and losing to your player?

Everyone understands physical and verbal abuse, but few parents realize the emotional abuse that children may go through in youth sports. Are you setting expectations that create undue pressure to perform? Unfortunately, many parents define being a winner by the outcome of their youth sports games. A win/loss record is always a poor measure of a player's overall success. It can create undue stress for both the players and the coaches. Remember, the opposing team's skill and ability isn't what determines whether your player is a winner or loser. Children and young adults will remember how the coaches and parents made them feel after a game, and the kids who continually work hard to perform up to their potential will more than likely find the rewards of winning.

Win the game as a parent, and set your kids up for success. Encourage your youth player to compete against themselves by continually improving. The main focus of youth baseball should be skill development and refinement. When players perform to their full potential but still lose the game, the game outcome is not a fair measure of success. As parents we should be working together to be supportive during the good and bad. Try not to continuously point out your child's mistakes.

Guilt and threats are not motivational tools and usually have psychological repercussions. Challenge your kids each and every day, and tell them you believe they can do it.

Help your child learn the difference between success and failure vs. winning and losing. Youth baseball and sports can be a microcosm of life. Kids can't simply expect to win. They have to work hard to earn it, and even then, there are no guarantees. All we can do is prepare and perform to the best of our ability to achieve what we desire in sports or in life. If you define success in terms of winning and losing, you're setting your player up for failure. If you truly want your child to succeed in life, give them the gift of failure and the tools to deal with it positively. I know that may sound confusing, but stop and think about it. If you teach your children how to view setbacks, mistakes, and risks, you'll be giving them the keys to a lifetime of success and opportunity.

As a long-time dedicated coach, I can tell you that no one takes more ownership and responsibility for a team's record than the coach. It weighs heavy on our hearts and minds if we can't deliver a win for our kids and their families. As a youth baseball coach, you're in a constant struggle every game to balance participation with winning, and encouragement with discipline—all the while knowing that if you coddle these kids, you will set them up for failure. We as coaches rely heavily on the parents to be a foundation of positive encouragement so we can do our jobs and still keep the kids motivated and excited.

For many, playing sports has been a rite of passage where children become young adults—and, yes, it involves winning and losing. However, youth baseball coaches should seldom measure their success or ability on a win/loss record. If you're a coach who has the patience and organization to teach discipline, fundamentals, focus, and hard work to improve individual players, you can be a good coach. Forget about the records or standings. And for every parent who isn't happy with the game outcome, I'll show you ten more who want to be on your team next year because of your positive coaching style.

Of course players like to win, but they also want a good experience. Young players need more encouragement and attention after losing a game. They need more discipline after a win as well. But pizza and soda always tend to help cope with both.

At the end of the day, the children like to know that you still approve and have faith in them, as a player and son or daughter. A game lost is forgotten, but hurt feelings are remembered. Love unconditionally, and promote self-esteem. Let them know what you saw was positive and express why that made you proud. Saying these five words, "I love watching you play," can go a long way.

Parents can help their kids reach their full potential by participating with them. Every coach knows which kids are practicing at home and which aren't. It's evident in their progress.

Players, parents, and coaches should support each other. Winning and losing should be diminished as a simple game outcome because it isn't the pinnacle of the youth sports experience. Teach the kids the game, and prepare them for the next level of baseball. In doing so, you'll prepare them for the next level in life. Focus on the process, not the outcome.

Focus on what you can control. In baseball, work, and life, there are so many things we can't control (e.g., what other people do and think, external factors, and ultimately the results), but we always have the choice to control our own attitude and effort. Remembering what you can or can't control and putting your attention on your attitude and efforts are key elements in staying focused, being positive, and reducing stress. In baseball, if you waste your time getting upset about the umpire's calls, the decisions your coaches make, the weather conditions, and more, you'll make yourself crazy and render yourself ineffective in the game. The same is true in life—we waste so much energy on stuff we have no control over. When we shift our focus as players, parents, and coaches to what we *can* control (our attitude and effort), we're empowered. You owe it to yourself to be the best you can possibly be—both in baseball and in life.

As I said in the beginning, my goal is to pass along this information because I am now at the stage in my life when giving back is really important. Because this information has helped me and others so much, I wanted to share it with all of you. It's up to you to decide how valuable the information is and how you choose to use it.

Of course, I believe this book will help you accomplish your own player, parent, and coaching goals. I hope it will help you to do it both individually and for others. And since your journey and evolution in all three phases will certainly be a struggle, I trust this information will help you struggle and evolve well.

Along these lines, there is more to come in the future—because I believe that a good plan, the right information, and the best tools all greatly contribute to helping people create lasting baseball memories. I will soon have more of that available to you.

RESOURCES AND SUGGESTED READING BOOKS

Dweck, Carole. *Mindset*. New York, NY: Ballantine Books, 2006.

Foer, Joshua. *Moonwalking with Einstein*. New York, NY: Penguin Books. 2011.

Johnson, Derek. *The Complete Guide to Pitching*. Champaign, IL: Human Kinetics. 2013.

Knight, Phil. *Shoe Dog*. New York, NY: Scribner—Simon & Schuster. 2016.

Law, Keith, *Smart Baseball*. New York, NY: HarperCollins Publishers, 2017.

Lewis, Michael L. *Moneyball: The Art of Winning an Unfair Game*. New York, NY: W. W. Norton & Company. 2004.

Matheny, Mike. *The Matheny Manifesto*. New York, NY: Crown Archetype. 2015.

Maxwell, John. *How Successful People Think*. New York, NY: Center Street. 2009.

Maxwell, John. *The 360 Leader*. Nashville, TN: Thomas Nelson. 2006.

McKey, Zoe. *Discipline Your Mind*. New York, NY: Independent Publishing. 2017.

O'Sullivan, John. *Changing the Game*. New York, NY: Morgan James Publishing, 2014.

Passan, Jeff. *The Arm*. New York, NY: HarperCollins. 2016.

Peck, Scott. M. *The Road Less Traveled*. New York, NY: Touchstone. 2003.

Peterson, Rick & Hoekstra. *Crunch Time*. Oakland, CA: Berrett-Koehler Publishers. 2017.

Ripken, Cal Jr. & Bill. *Coaching Youth Baseball the Ripken Way*. Champaign, IL: Human Kinetics. 2007.

Ryan & House, Nolan & Tom. *Nolan Ryan's Pitcher's Bible*. New York, NY: Simon & Schuster/Fireside. 1991.

Tracy, Brian. *No Excuses*. Boston, MA: MJF Books. 2010.

Verducci, Tom. *The Cubs Way*. New York, NY: Crown Publishing Group. 2017.

Williams, Ted. *The Science of Hitting*. New York, NY: Touchstone. 1970 / 2013.

WEBSITES

Here is a list of websites I use as a coach for drills, rules, and other valuable information:

Babe Ruth Baseball - www.baberuthleague.org

Babe Ruth Coaching Education - www.baberuthcoaching.org

Baseball Almanac - www.baseball-almanac.com

Baseball Tutorials - www.baseball-tutorials.com

Coach Baseball Right - https://coachbaseballright.com/

CoachTube - https://coachtube.com/

Little League Baseball and Softball - www.littleleague.org

National Alliance for Youth Sports - www.nays.com

QCBaseball - www.qcbaseball.com

Ripken Baseball - www.ripkenbaseball.com

USA Baseball - www.usabaseball.com

SOCIAL MEDIA

www.facebook.com/joey.anderson.1654

http://twitter.com/JoeyandersonTc

www.instagram.com/joeyanderson9362

EMAIL ADDRESS

joeyanderson1220@gmail.com

ABOUT THE AUTHOR

Joey Anderson was born in Galesburg, Illinois, on December 20, 1977, and moved to Roseburg, Oregon, in 1981, where he grew up a very ordinary, middle-class kid. He enjoys reading, writing, traveling, coaching baseball, and spending time with friends and family.

For the past eighteen years, he has been an industrial sales manager in both Oregon and California. Along the way, he earned numerous awards for excellence in the areas of sales, personnel, and finance. He believes that his success isn't due to anything special about him—it is the result of the life lessons and experiences he has acquired through hard work, dedication, making mistakes, learning from them, and growing to become a better person.

He has spent the past thirty years playing baseball, being a parent, and coaching youth baseball. Joey has coached Little League, Babe Ruth Baseball, all stars, and travel teams. He is a Babe Ruth Baseball certified coach and a current member of the American Baseball Coaches Association.

He currently lives in the Umpqua River Valley with his fiancée and kids. *The Triple Crown of Youth Baseball* is his first book.

Made in the USA
San Bernardino, CA
15 June 2018